How

Money

Learn How to Save Up to 5000$ per year

Wilton Jerrard

HOW TO SAVE MONEY

Table of Contents

INTRODUCTION **4**

CHAPTER 01..**5**

CHAPTER 02 ....**9**

CHAPTER 03 ....**21**

CHAPTER 04 ....**32**

CHAPTER 05 ....**37**

CHAPTER 06 ....**45**

CHAPTER 07 ....**49**

CHAPTER 08 ....**52**

CHAPTER 09 ....**58**

CHAPTER 10...**64**

CONCLUSION **69**

Introduction

This book describes the benefits of saving money. Discussing about the formulas to save 5000$ or more step by step in seven steps. If your approach is towards saving money then this is book tells about the ways you can save money and if your approach is towards earning 5000$ extra in a year then this book will help you with giving ideas according to that approach. It tells you the guidelines to follow during the process and the blunders to avoid during the process as well.

This indeed is a great book which will help you in saving a lot of money in the long run so you can use that money for your retirement plan or any adventure.

Chapter 01

Importance of saving money

Saving money necessitates a great deal of self-control. It is, however, a habit that may be easily formed with firm commitment and the establishment of financial goals. Many Singaporeans can considerably benefit from the practice of saving if they chose to do so consistently.

Some of the benefits of saving money are described below:

1. Assists in emergencies: Emergencies happen at any time. So, when they rise, the necessary monies are frequently not included in the regular budget. There will be pressure to find additional funding on short notice. If the emergency involves a sudden sickness or vehicle accident, the matter can become even worse. It might be a life-or-death situation. Savings can help to alleviate the problem. The appropriate treatment will be given to the patient right away. Funeral bills, urgent house repairs, and even car maintenance are examples of other crises that could be covered by savings. However, such situations normally necessitate a substantial number of moneys.

2. Protects against job loss: Losing a job is always painful. It can put a family in a lot of trouble. When faced with an unexpected loss of income, saving can be a wonderful source of consolation. When one is out of work, it is usually exceedingly difficult to borrow money. As a result, people who have not been sensible enough to save will be absolutely broke after losing their work.

HOW TO SAVE MONEY

3. Assists with the funding of vacations: Many Singaporeans wish to take a holiday at least once a year. However, due to a shortage of funding, this is usually not achievable. Savings can enable you to realize your ambition of taking a holiday. A time of rest, relaxation, and bonding can be shared by family and friends.

4. Helps to limit debt: Having some money set aside can assist in limiting one's debt burden. Instead of using a credit card, you might utilize your savings to pay for some expenses. This will significantly reduce the amount of debt owed as well as the amount of money that may have been spent on interest. Savings also allow you to avoid taking out emergency loans in the event of an emergency, allowing you to reduce your debt even more.

5. Provides financial freedom: Savings provide peace of mind and enable one to experience financial freedom. Knowing that there is a buffer that can be used if money is required urgently is reassuring. This is in contrast to individuals who live paycheck to paycheck. If an unforeseen expense occurs, they are suddenly financially stranded.

6. Assists with retirement planning: There are long-term advantages to saving. One of them is having sufficient retirement funds. Many retirees who rely on a pension do not have enough money to cover all of their expenses. Over the course of several years, saving a little portion of one's income can add up to a significant amount of retirement savings. This will make retirement a lot more pleasant. Most people find it difficult to save money for retirement all too often. This is due to the unknowns of the future, such as whether or not you will be living to spend the money. Despite this, it is prudent to consider conserving money that

may be useful to your beneficiaries if you are unable to spend it.

Begin today by identifying some of the most effective strategies to save money. You may, for example, begin by selling some of the stuff you no longer use. You can save money by selling your Rolex at today's best pricing. Have a savings goal in mind, and figure out how much money you can spare to help you reach it.

It's also a good idea to consider boosting your savings rate from time to time. You might not be able to do so at first, and that's okay. However, as time passes, be willing to increase the percentage rate, no matter how tiny it is.

7. Assists with the financing of higher education: Higher education fees are a significant expense in Singapore. Savings will allow you to continue your study without having to look for money elsewhere. This will allow you to advance swiftly in your job. This is advantageous for those who are not eligible for a personal loan or an education loan.

8. Assists in the financing of a home down payment:

Putting money aside can be the first step toward becoming a proud homeowner. Before a mortgage application can be granted, all banks require a down payment of a particular proportion. It is impossible to borrow the amount to be put down as a deposit. As a result, the person will have to get it from his or her own funds or from family and friends. Because family and friends may not have the necessary finances, saving will be a better option.

9. Assists in the financing of a wedding: Weddings are a significant expense in Singapore. Because to financial

restraints, many couples have to postpone their wedding. The couple may plan their wedding day with confidence now that they have amassed savings.

Chapter 02

Save Money Step by Step

And I'll teach you how to accomplish it in detail — step by step.

Let's get started.

1. Dedication

I'm going to presume you're reading this because you:

Would you like to save $5000?

It's difficult for me to do so.

You've come to the proper location if those two statements are correct. However, this implies that in order to attain your $5000 target, you'll have to approach things differently than you have in the past.

Are you ready to adapt new situations? It is difficult to change. It's only human that a part of us opposes change. Anticipate your own apprehension.

That means you must be 100 percent devoted to achieving your objective, even if the changes we're going to discuss make you uncomfortable. As a result, I'll ask you again:

Are you willing to do something new, even if it makes you uncomfortable, in order to save $5000 in the next year?

Let's move on to step 2 if you replied "yes."

2. Your Alternatives

There are three ways to save $5000:

• Spend less money.

HOW TO SAVE MONEY

- Make more money.

- It's a mix of the two.

You probably already know which of these selections is the best fit for you.

If you look around and realize that you make the same amount of money as or more than most of the people around you but can't save a dollar, it's time to start lowering your expenditures. (Don't be concerned.) We'll talk about how to achieve it.)

Tip 1: Consider driving for a rideshare service to supplement your income during your free time. If you do that, you may be able to meet your $5000 goal rather soon.

Cutting expenditure is unlikely if you make far less than the majority of people in your circumstance. Simply said, you need to earn more money. (Again, we'll go over how to do it in a minute.)

Here's another easy technique to figure out where you should put your concentration. Take a look at the graph below. This shows how much money you'll need to save each month, week, and day to meet your $5000 target in 12 months.

Month: 416.67$

Week: 96.15$

Day: 13.89$

HOW TO SAVE MONEY

Are you able to save $13.89 every day or $96 per week with ease? If that's the case, the most straightforward way to achieve your aim is to reduce expenditure.

If it appears to be an insurmountable endeavor, you'll need to boost your income.

If a hybrid strategy appears to be the best option, that's acceptable as well.

3. Baby Drill

It's time to get down to business. We'll go over all of the actual measures you have available to help you achieve, determine which to take first, and then get started.

Assume you need to boost your monthly revenue by $416.67 dollars.

To meet your objective if you earn $20 per hour, you'll need to work around 30 more hours each month (after taxes).

That's a total of 7 to 12 hours every week. Is it possible for you to work longer hours?

If not, are you able to find a part-time job? Starting a side business appeals to me as well. This could be an excellent movie, but it may take some time for the money to start flowing in. We want to see the tangible results as soon as possible.

Make the greatest decision that will result in quick outcomes.

A tiny side business could be fantastic, but if it doesn't result in savings next month, put it on your "to-do" list for the time being.

The other option is to reduce your monthly spending by $416.

HOW TO SAVE MONEY

4. Strike It

We've considered all of the options and determined which is the best to execute. Now is the time to get started. I am confident in your ability to complete this task and succeed.

If you've made it this far, you're serious about becoming $50000 richer in the next 12 months. You already know what to do. Now let's get started. Set up a $416.67 monthly auto-debit from your checking account you'll save your $5000 over the next year.

This is a crucial phase since it puts pressure on you to succeed. All you have to do now is come up with the necessary funds and/or increasing earnings. You do not have an option!

5. Monthly Monitoring

The final step is accountability, which ensures that you stay on course. First thing to do is to enlist the help of a trustworthy buddy as an accountability partner.

Discuss your annual and monthly objectives with her, as well as what you plate reason n to do to achieve them.

Wise to update her on your progress each month by providing proof that you have saved the $416.

You will face problems whenever you embark on a meaningful trip. However, if you follow each of these procedures, you will achieve your goal.

You'll be able to move on to larger and better things after you reach this $5000 target. From here, the sky is the limit.

HOW TO SAVE MONEY

Want to Save five thousand dollars in a Year in 7 Simple Steps:

1. Figure out the reason why you want to save $5,000 in the first place

Knowing why 're saving $5,000 or any amount of money makes it easier to motivate yourself to do so.

Listed below are a few examples:

Are you attempting to save money in order to purchase a car?

Do you want to put money aside for a property down payment?

Do you want to pay off your student loans more quickly?

Once you've figured out what your "why" is, write it down so you don't forget.

Here's an illustration: I've written down my aim of saving $5,000 by 2020 to replace my air conditioner on a post-it note.

Every time I open that closet, I'll be reminded of the aim.

2. Create a new bank account just for this challenge.

Second step is to open a bank account expressly for this challenge after you've determined why you want to save $5,000.

Keeping the money separate makes it easy to track your progress.

CIT Bank and Discover Bank are where I do my banking. Both online banks have substantially higher interest rates than the national average.

HOW TO SAVE MONEY

Savings accounts at many internet banks feature no fees or minimums.

When you open your new account, your bank may allow you to give it a unique name, such as "Save $5,000 in 2020."

3. Go through your budget from the previous month.

Now that you've completed the organization tasks, take a few minutes to analyze your budget from the previous month.

What if you don't have a budget? Instead, go through your bank and credit card statements.

Go over each of your budget categories one by one for this review. Make a list of areas where you might be able to save money.

Overspending is common in the following categories:

•   Groceries

•   Restaurants   &   Take-Out   Entertainment Subscriptions & Memberships Cell Phone Transportation

•   Shopping for other things

I underlined the following categories when reviewing my budget: Subscriptions and Memberships, as well as groceries and transportation.

Continue reading when you've made a list of areas where you can improve...

4. Establish Expense-Reduction and Income-Increment Goals

HOW TO SAVE MONEY

Setting goals is the focus of the fourth step. If you want to save $5,000 over the course of a year, you only have a few options:

• Spend less money

• Boost your earnings

• a mixture of both

You may not have much spending room left if you've already cut your cable TV in half and moved to a $25/month cell phone plan.

After all, to meet your $5,000 objective, you'll need to save $417 per month.

Here's what I'd recommend: Using the list from the third stage, make a goal to reduce spending, then make a second objective to increase income.

I intend to save $4,000 while increasing my income by $1,000.

After all, to meet your $5,000 objective, you'll need to save $417 per month.

Here's what I'd recommend: Using the list from the third stage, make a goal to reduce spending, then make a second objective to increase income.

I intend to save $4,000 while increasing my income by $1,000.

Putting some numbers on paper isn't enough to save $5,000 in a year. You'll need a strategy. I'm going to share mine with you in the hopes of inspiring you to make your own.

Zohaib's Action Plan: $5,000 in a Year of Savings

Expense Reduction: $4,000 in 12 months

HOW TO SAVE MONEY

Cancel food delivery, continue twice-weekly meal preparation, and limit store excursions.

Consolidate trips, use toll lanes sparingly, and utilize the free trolley instead of Uber.

Memberships: Canceled unlimited spin in favor of a cheaper

ClassPass plan; for at-home exercises, use a $99 annual Beachbody subscription.

Increase your income by $1,000 over the course of a year.

Only when redeemed for cash back can credit card rewards be used (not points or miles)

Ibotta and Fetch Rewards are two grocery rebate apps.

Online shopping cashback portals: Rakuten & Topcashback

Make money online by completing MTurk assignments if necessary to obtain a monthly income of $83.

5. Invested in Your Savings Account on a Regular Basis

Defined up transfers from your checking account to your savings account now that you've set goals and made an action plan.

Here are two ways to get to $5,000 a year (or $417 per month) in a year:

Set up automatic transfers to be made every month or pay period.

Manual transfers: As you make success in cutting spending and boosting revenue, set up one-time transfers.

Although automatic transfers are more convenient, manual transfers should not be discounted. They were effective for me.

HOW TO SAVE MONEY

I started with automated transfers and gradually added manual transfers to attain my goal of paying off my mortgage in two years.

Automatic transfer did not do it this way, I found that taking two minutes to log into my bank account and set up a manual payment kept me motivated and reminded me of my progress.

Manual transfers may also be the ideal option if you can save money on a major item, such as housing, and make significant progress in only one transfer.

I also recommend them for sporadic revenue, such as side hustles and online earning.

6. Recognize and reward your accomplishments along the way

Next, while you work toward saving $5,000 in a year, reward yourself for your accomplishments. This is an important step.

Consider a few ways to reward yourself for your accomplishments to keep yourself motivated.

Here's an example: I'm going to get tacos at this establishment down the block every month transfer more than $417 to the savings account. Although the dinner is just approximately $12, I don't go there very often because it is not on my diet. In that sense, it's a "treat" in more ways than one. To keep things interesting, I might try new restaurants.

For this challenge, reward yourself with a cup of coffee, a movie ticket, or some other little prize for each month you stay on track to save $5,000 in a year.

7. Share your goal with a close family member or friend.

HOW TO SAVE MONEY

Finally, having a support system will make attaining your goal of saving $5,000 in a year, or any goal in life, much easier. Speak with a family member or a close friend.

Have a talk with your spouse about this challenge if you have one.

Obviously, if you have joint bank accounts with someone, you must agree on your financial goals.

Even if you're single, I believe it's a good thing to inform your family and friends.

Tell your friends about your intentions to save $5,000 in a year, why it's essential to you, and how they can help.

For most people, saving money is a priority, but it needs discipline. It can be beneficial to have a strategy or a program to follow to boost your chances of achieving your financial objectives.

You'll discover a free printable chart in this post that demonstrates how to save $5,000 in a year by putting aside a tiny amount each week. You will also find a load of advice and practical suggestions for cutting costs and saving money.

$5,000 may seem like a lot of money to save, and it is, but it works out for less than $100 per week over the course of a year. When you put it like way, it sounds a lot more reasonable.

You'll reach $5,000 in a year if you follow the approach outlined in this article, and the most that you will save in any given week will be $130.

What Would You Do If You Were Given $5,000?

HOW TO SAVE MONEY

$5,000 is a substantial sum of money. There are a variety of things you can do with it.

• Set aside money for retirement.

• Have a wonderful vacation.

• It can be used to make a down payment on a home.

• Purchase a low-cost used car or put the money toward a more expensive vehicle.

• Create an emergency fund.

I'm sure you'll have no trouble coming up with a few suggestions. In fact, you could already have a precise idea in mind.

What is the point of a savings challenge?

While a money-saving challenge isn't required to save money, it can help in a variety of ways.

It's a blast

Let's be honest: saving money isn't always fun. Sure, seeing the benefits is exciting, but saving money requires dedication and sacrifice.

A financial challenge can make a dull subject more interesting and pleasurable. You'll be more inclined to persist with saving if you make it enjoyable.

Accountability

Even if it's only accountability to oneself, the savings challenge offers some accountability. Hopefully, once you start the challenge, you'll feel compelled to finish it.

You can set a general goal of saving money, but the money challenge provides you specific weekly savings objectives that you can track at any moment.

HOW TO SAVE MONEY

Competition

Why not team up with a friend to take on a savings challenge? Taking the challenge with a friend increases your accountability and provides additional motivation due to the competition.

It's possible that the competition isn't about who saves the most money if you stick to the plan and the stated amounts to save. Instead, it's more about sticking with the challenge and seeing it through. Most of us don't want to see a friend finish a challenge that we gave up on, so it provides added drive to complete it.

Do not worry about the math.

One of the appealing aspects of the challenge is that it handles the math for you. All you need to do is to deposit the amount mentioned on the printout each week, and after 52 weeks, you'll have $5,000.

For the Challenge, I'm going to open a new savings account.

I propose keeping a separate savings account for the challenge, even if it isn't strictly necessary. The following are the two key reasons:

You'll be able to check how much money you've saved at any given time.

It's simple to keep the money separate from your other accounts so you don't withdraw the money you're saving for the challenge by accident.

Chapter 03

Several Options for Saving $5,000

So, now that you have the printable, you can plan out how much money you'll save each week. That's fantastic, but if you're living paycheck to paycheck, you might be wondering where you'll get the money to save each week. Let us look at some of things you can do to free up money to put in your savings account with that in mind.

1. Make a financial plan

This is first things you should think about if you don't already have one. A budget will assist you in making the most of every dollar and allowing you to live comfortably within your means. Your budget will outline how you intend to spend your money, as well as how much you aim to save or invest.

2. Keep tabs on your spending

It's great to have a budget, but you won't know whether you're actually keeping to it until you track your costs as well. I recommend keeping track of your expenses every day so you don't lose track, and you'll be able to see precisely how much you're spending and what you're spending it on at the end of the month.

Tracking your spending might help you identify areas where you may be overspending. You can pinpoint the places where you're squandering money. Once know that, you may make adjustments to your expenditure to address those difficulties, resulting in additional money saved.

I've always found that tracking your spending drives you to evaluate every purchase, and you'll be much more careful with your money if you know you'll be keeping track of it.

HOW TO SAVE MONEY

It's one of the most beneficial things you can do for your own finances.

3. Save Money on Your Phone Bill

How much do you pay on your cell phone or wireless service each month? If you are with one of the major carriers, switching to a reduced pre-paid carrier might save you hundreds of dollars per year.

My wife and I switched from the top carriers to a reduced carrier (Boost Mobile) about 8 years ago, and our cost was promptly slashed in half. We used to pay $140 per month for the two of us, but now we just pay $70 per month. That's an annual savings of $840!

We went from Boost to Cricket Wireless about 4 years ago. We're still paying $70 a month, but our coverage is significantly better in our neighborhood. Cricket operates on the AT&T network; however, coverage is available with very low-cost cell phone contracts. Cricket has been a great experience for me, and I highly suggest them.

Switching to a reduced carrier has been one of the simplest ways I've ever saved money, and it saves me money every month. I was initially apprehensive about the service's quality, but this has not been an issue.

4. Cut the Cable or Satellite TV Cord

Another simple way my wife and I saved money was by discontinuing cable television. I haven't missed it since we cancelled it approximately 8 years ago. We now watch a lot of episodes and movies on Netflix, thanks to an HD antenna I bought for less than $50. During football season, I also subscribe to Sling in order to watch ESPN stations.

Even with the Sling membership, we save a significant amount of money each month. We save a lot of money every month/year because Netflix is our sole TV-related bill for the majority of the year.

5. Spend Less on Food

Food is a large line item in most budgets, and there are many methods to cut down on your monthly food spending. If you eat a lot of meals out or buy your lunch at work every day, switching to making all (or almost all) of your meals at home can save you a lot of money.

You don't have to skip restaurants totally, but you should limit the number of meals you eat out and keep track of how much money you spend when you do. My essay on how to save money at restaurants may be of use.

Almost certainly, your grocery bill may be cut without any effort as well. Shopping at inexpensive grocery stores like Aldi is my favorite way to save money on food. Our family of four saves a few thousand dollars every year thanks to Aldi's inexpensive prices and generic brands. Other options can be found in my article on how to save money on groceries.

6. Save Money Easily by Using Cash Back Apps

Utilizing cashback applications is one of my favorite methods to save money. There are a plethora of websites and apps that allow you to earn cash back on a variety of transactions, but here are three of my favorites.

Rakuten ($10 registration bonus) — A free Rakuten account can save you money on most online purchases as well as some in-store purchases. Rakuten partners with thousands of retailers and websites, and you profit by receiving cash back on purchases you would have made anyway.

Rakuten offers a browser extension that makes saving really simple. When you use the extension, you'll receive a notification whenever you visit a website that offers

HOW TO SAVE MONEY

Rakuten cashback. All you need, is to activate your shopping trip by clicking a button, and you'll be ready to save money. Rakuten will even search and apply promo codes for you to save even more money.

Ibotta ($20 in signup incentives) - Ibotta is a fantastic cashback program that can help you save money at grocery stores, department stores, house improvement stores, and other retailers, as well as online. Offers are available for a wide range of products and retailers, and you may choose which ones you want to use.

TopCashback - TopCashback is a cashback site that is very similar to Rakuten. You can save money with thousands of their partner websites with a free account. I recommend that you sign up for both Rakuten and TopCashback because the deal may be better at Rakuten at times and at TopCashback at other times (or cashback may be available only through one of them).

7. Sign-up bonuses and rewards for credit cards

Taking advantage of credit card offers is another simple approach to locate extra money to save. Sign up for new credit card and you can earn you anywhere from $100 to $1,000 as a one-time bonus. On all of their purchases, you can earn cash back or travel rewards.

I get anywhere from 2% to 5% reward on every purchase by using a couple of different credit cards. If you make all of the purchases with a credit card, this easily adds up over the course of a year (with no change in your lifestyle).

8. Find a Cheaper Insurance Policy

Have you looked around for a better deal on insurance? The majority of us have multiple insurance policies (auto, life, home/renters, and health). It's possible that you may save money by switching to a different company or making some changes to your current policy.

HOW TO SAVE MONEY

You can double-check your current coverage to ensure you're not over insured. By lowering the coverage for our belongings, we were able to save more than $100 each year on our homeowner's insurance. We didn't require as much coverage as we already had. Increasing your deductible can also help you save money on your insurance costs.

9. Get rid of anything you do not need.

We have a lot of things we don't use or need lying around the house. While some of it may appear to be trash, much of it has worth. Going through your house and selecting items to sell is one of the simplest methods to get some extra cash.

If you have enough items, you may hold a yard sale to swiftly get rid of them. Last year, my wife and I made over $400 from a weekend yard sale, and we're going to have more this year.

Although yard sales are fantastic for getting rid of a lot in a day or two, selling your precious stuff elsewhere will certainly net you more money. Both Facebook Marketplace and Craigslist are wonderful resources for quickly reaching a large number of individuals.

10. Save Money on Entertainment

Entertainment is one of the areas of the budget where many people may make big savings by cutting back. How much do you spend on entertainment? Outings to the movies, sporting events, and concerts, as well as trips to the bar and lunches out with friends, may quickly add up.

This isn't to imply you shouldn't spend money on entertainment. While we spend time with family and friends doing activities you enjoy is a terrific way to pass the time, there are methods to save money on entertainment without compromising enjoyment. Find free or low-cost activities to do, adopt a low-cost hobby, or set a strict limit on your spending on the entertainment.

11. Begin a side business

While cutting costs is beneficial, increasing your income can help you save more quickly. There are many side hustle ideas to choose from that you're bound to find something that works for you. Here are a handful of my favorite ways to rapidly earn additional cash.

Flea Market Flipping - I just mentioned the option of selling items you no longer use. By buying and reselling, you may convert this into a side venture that pays out on a regular basis. Items can be purchased through yard sales, thrift stores, and flea markets and then resold for a profit.

Pet Sitting and Dog Walking - You might be amazed how much money you can make as a side hustle by pet sitting or dog walking. I was surprised to learn that Lily's home-based doggy daycare earns her $40,000+ a year when I interviewed her on how to become a pet sitter. On Rover, you may establish a profile and allow clients to find you (Lily gets all of her clients from Rover). One of the best things about this side hustle is that it doesn't require any specific expertise.

Freelancing - You can earn extra money by providing a variety of services as a freelancer. Freelance writing is my favorite because there are so many blogs and websites that need content on a regular basis.

Drive for Door Dash - Working as a delivery driver might help you supplement your income regardless of your existing work schedule. Driving for Door Dash offers a lot of flexibility in terms of earning money.

Take Paid Internet Surveys - Taking paid online surveys is one of the most popular side hustles. It isn't the most lucrative alternative, but it is quite flexible, and you can complete surveys while watching TV or anytime you have free time. Few survey websites:

Swagbucks ($5 incentive when you sign up)

Inbox Dollars ($5 bonus when you sign up)

My Points

Survey Junkie ($10 signup bonus)

12. Your Thermostat Should Be Adjusted

Despite a 1.8 percent decrease in home electricity rates in 2019, the average monthly energy bill in the United States remains approximately $115, with heating and cooling accounting for 43% of this expenditure, according to the Energy Information Administration. Although you won't be able to avoid this expense entirely, you can save money by just adjusting your thermostat. According to the US Energy Department, lowering the thermostat by 7 to 10 degrees for eight hours a day will save you 10% on your annual energy cost.

13. Cut the cord

According to NationWide.com, the average monthly cost of basic cable is $60, with premium channels costing substantially more. However, according to John Schmoll, publisher of FrugalRules.com and former U.S. News contributor, there are various streaming alternatives to explore that can reduce those prices.

Sling TV, which offers a variety of major channels like HGTV, ESPN, and CNN for $35 per month, is a good option for those who aren't ready to give up their beloved cable shows. If you switch from basic cable to this streaming service, you'll save $25 a month on entertainment, and even more if you subscribe for premium sports or movie channels.

HOW TO SAVE MONEY

14. Increase the Deductible on Your Auto Insurance

Saving money on insurance doesn't have to mean compromising coverage. In fact, increasing your deductible on your auto insurance coverage will save you money right away. According to data gathered by CarInsurance.com, increasing your deductible from $250 to $1,000 can save you $30 per month.

Jim Wang recommends putting the money you save each month into a separate online savings account when lowering your insurance deductible. This manner, he claims, you'll be insured in the event of a repair.

Meanwhile, to save money, Cameron Huddleston, recommends paying in full rather than monthly. "Ask your insurer whether they give this discount; it's a fairly popular one." Simply save aside enough money each month to cover the whole cost when it's due," she advises.

15. Get a Bonus When You Sign Up

Don't just use any credit card; choose one that will help you get the most cash back on every purchase.

"Using the correct card can make a tremendous difference," says Trae Budge, a smart buying guru and former U.S. News contributor at TrueTrae.com. She suggests using Giga Points, a free platform that analyses your credit card usage and suggests the best cards for you based on your past purchases. "Just last year, the site showed me that I could have earned about $2,000 more in prizes."

16. Get rid of your unused gym membership.

Signing up to use a training facility is usually a good idea, but many gym subscriptions are a waste of money. According to the Statistic Brain Research Institute, the average cost of a gym membership is roughly $58 per month, with 67% of such contracts leaving unused. Even if you enjoy coming to the gym but are concerned about your safety, you may still be paying a monthly fee.

"Review your gym membership terms to make sure you're not paying to have your membership suspended," says Juan Carlos Cruz, founder of Brightwater Financial Group in Brooklyn, New York.

"Because of the wide variety of fitness programs and channels available, YouTube is the ideal source for free videos." It provides a variety of free fitness channels that would cost hundreds, if not thousands of dollars at a gym. "There are also videos for people of all levels of experience," Cruz adds. "Because of the wide variety of fitness programs and channels available, YouTube is the ideal source for free videos." It provides a variety of free fitness channels that would cost hundreds, if not thousands of dollars at a gym. "There are also videos for people of all levels of experience," Cruz adds.

17. Reduce your reliance on takeout

Food delivery apps have exploded in popularity, with more Americans than ever ordering meals through services like Uber Eats, DoorDash, and Postmates. Considering that the typical DoorDash customer spends $36.95 each order, according to Slice Intelligence data, cutting back on just a one takeout order per month would save you a lot of money. Just make sure you're preparing in quantity and storing leftovers so you'll always have a quick-to-reheat dinner on hand.

18. Reduce Food Waste

Food waste is not just bad for the environment; it's also bad for our wallets. The average American household throws out $1,866 in uneaten groceries each year. Although totally eliminating food waste will take time, there are a few basic strategies you can start using right now to save money and groceries.

Shelly Longenecker, author of "Dinner for a Dollar," recommends performing a "fridge check." "A fridge check is when you check your refrigerator every few days for two to three minutes to see if anything needs to be used up before it goes bad," says the author "she explains. "This easy step allows you to save food and find a use for it before it has to be thrown away."

Meanwhile, preparing a few weekly meals ahead of time with similar items will help to reduce food waste.

19. Make the switch to a no-fee banking account.

When it comes to saving money, bank fees can cut into your efforts, with average monthly checking account maintenance fees hanging around $14.39, according to a Money Rates report from 2020.

There are lots of free possibilities, according to Simon Zhen, a research analyst for financial services comparison site MyBankTracker.com and former U.S. News contributor. "A consumer can avoid paying any monthly cost by moving to a free checking account, such as those frequently offered by internet banks," he explains.

20. Organize a Babysitting Co-op for Parents

Any parent will tell you that babysitter expenses add up quickly. You could need a sitter for a weeknight or weekend in addition to daycare while you're at work. According to the 2019 Care.com Cost of Care Survey, the average babysitting rate is $16.25 per hour, so going out without the kids for four hours once a month will cost you an extra $780 per year in child care.

Violette de Ayala, founder, and CEO of FemCity, a professional women's networking organization, says you can save money by organizing a babysitting co-op with other parents in your neighborhood or through your children's school. "It generates an instant play date for the kids and saves parents money on a sitter's hourly charge," she explains.

Chapter 04

Now we are going to discuss the ways to make an extra 5000$ very fast.

Although it may appear to be a difficult effort, it is feasible to make $5,000 in a short period of time.

We tend to conceive of things in 52-week cycles, but earning $5,000 doesn't have to take a full year. Working an extra few hours per week can get you there in less than a year, or even faster if you devote more time to it.

But, for you, is "months" even too long?

In the meantime, here's some advice before you get started: When it comes to building a side hustle, don't strive to be too broad.

1. Get behind the wheel.

By driving for a ridesharing service like Lyft or Uber, you can turn a depreciating asset — your car — into an income-producing asset.

Clark Howard, a financial specialist, tried both Uber and Lyft. He made $57 before tax after driving for 4.5 hours in metro Atlanta.

That works out to $12.66 per hour on average. To earn $5,000 before taxes, you'd have to work 395 hours over the course of a year — or approximately 8 hours per week for 50 weeks.

2. Turn Your Phone's Pictures into Cash

If you're a photographer, this is fantastic news! There are a few of apps that will allow you to transform the photos on your smartphone into cash.

HOW TO SAVE MONEY

Snapwire, for example, is one of several apps that allows users to accept commissioned jobs (sometimes known as "requests" and "challenges") from businesses and ad agencies to photograph specific subjects. You can also sell your own portfolio of general interest photographs.

Snapwire deducts nothing from the sale price of requests and challenges, but a 50% fee is deducted from the sale price of portfolio photos that sell.

According to one recent study, the average photo in the requests and challenges category sells for between $50 and $75.

Other similar services include:

- Dreamstime

- eye

- Foap

- miPic (iOS only)

- ScoopShot

- Twenty20

3. Look for a job that allows you to work from home.

It may not be your cup of tea to run about town taking pictures or picking up the strangers in your car and having to make small talk.

You may attempt a work-at-home job if you like something a little more sedentary and predictable. While there are many different sorts of remote employment, customer service and virtual call center jobs are two of the most prominent.

Home agents can earn anything from $8 to $20 per hour, but a decent average is $9 to $15 per hour.

HOW TO SAVE MONEY

Many of these positions will require you to pass background and credit checks, and almost all of them will ask you to have a dedicated landline phone number that you exclusively use for work.

4. Wrap your car:

Wrapify will pay you to advertise firms on the go by wrapping the exterior of your vehicle in a branded wrap.

You simply drive your normal commute once you've been wrapped. Drivers are compensated per mile based on a visibility algorithm that takes into account the time of day and regions of heavy traffic.

According to Wrapify's website, a full wrap can earn you between $264 and $452 every month.

Partial wraps pay less per month, around $200. Do you only want to wrap one panel of your car? Every 30 days, you can expect to make between $84 and $140.

5. Take on unusual jobs

There are numerous opportunities to earn some extra income by doing odd chores around your neighborhood.

If you want to add a modern twist to this path, go to TaskRabbit and sign up for odd jobs in your region. Tasks range from housecleaning to errand running, and you'll be paid an hourly rate for your efforts.

IKEA has also teamed up with TaskRabbit to make it easier to hire "taskers" to build furniture, mount it, or install lighting.

Again, it's difficult to pinpoint exactly what you need to do to earn $5,000 more. It all depends on what kind of odd job you do and how much you charge.

HOW TO SAVE MONEY

6. Sell Your (Or Someone Else's) Stuff

Many people have entire houses filled with things they don't desire, need, or use. While you probably won't be able to conduct a garage sale every week at your home, you can start with one huge sale and see where it takes you.

After you've decluttered your personal belongings, consider assisting others you know in decluttering their houses. Consider pitching yourself as an organizing consultant like Marie Kondo after you've had a few successful gigs under your belt.

In exchange for a share of the overall proceeds, you can offer to collect items that clients no longer desire and conduct a yard sale.

Consider "flipping" big-ticket products that you can get for cheap on Craigslist or Goodwill.

It's incredible how a little TLC can change old and discarded furniture — and how a little work to refurbish an old piece can bring in a handsome return.

7. Instruct Others

Teaching a skill or specialized information that you know to others is a terrific way to give back to your community while also making a little additional money. You get to give something useful to the people around you while also getting paid for your time.

To earn extra money, you can teach people in a variety of ways, including:

Tutoring Organize a workshop, lecture, seminar, or webinar

Writing in a field you know a lot about for print or online publications (i.e. gardening, mechanics, fitness, etc.)

HOW TO SAVE MONEY

It is important to remember that you do not have to try all of these possibilities. Simply choose the option that best suits with your needs. Building a website or blog isn't for everyone, and it takes a lot of effort before you start seeing a financial return. But they're all things to think about.

Teachers who can offer an educational program of some kind can earn $150 or more per student who attends. Tutors can earn up to $50 per hour.

Bloggers can easily earn a full-time income from their efforts, with freelance writers charging anything from $50 to $150 each piece depending on experience.

Chapter 05

When it comes to conserving money, there are five major blunders to avoid.

Saving money usually boils down to one thing: achieving financial freedom. While the term may have varied connotations for different people, it essentially refers to having control over your own life and decisions.

When you first begin saving, make sure you have a plan in place to ensure that you're prioritizing particular goals and that you're appropriately prepared for each of them.

1. You don't have an emergency fund.

If you're just getting started with saving, an emergency fund is the ideal place to start.

Many people are unaware about how damaging an emergency may be to their money until it is too late. In reality, over two-thirds of Americans, including 46% of the wealthiest households, lack the funds to cover a $500 auto repair or a $1,000 emergency room cost. Consider what could happen if you lost your work and had no savings to meet your basic necessities.

Having two separate emergency funds: any day fund and an emergency fund, is the best method to save for unexpected financial shocks.

A rainy-day fund is called the money that you can use to pay an unforeseen expense, such as a medical bill, from time to time.

The word "emergency fund" refers to a larger, longer-term savings account. This money should be sufficient to cover at least three to six months' worth of living expenses in an event that you are unable to work for any reason.

HOW TO SAVE MONEY

Start by going over your budget and identifying areas where you may save money. You might be able to save a few hundred dollars per month after reducing some expenses and eliminating others that aren't required.

2. Keeping emergency funds in a difficult-to-reach location

When it comes to emergency savings, you'll want to keep the funds in a readily accessible account, such as a savings account. If you put the money in a long-term investment account, such as a retirement account, or even a shorter-term investing account, you risk paying exorbitant costs if you need to withdraw it before a certain date.

If you set it as an automatic deduction from your paycheck, the money will be taken out before you have a chance to spend it, which will not only allow you to save more over time, but it will also help you build better habits and learn to live on less.

Not only for emergency savings, but for all your savings goals. If you plan to buy a property in the near future, make sure to deposit your money in a safe place where you won't be tempted to spend it on frivolous things. When it's time to make that down payment, you'll thank yourself

So, once you've established your savings accounts, set up direct deposit so that a certain amount of money is being deducted from each paycheck and deposited directly into each account. You'll be able to see your money begin to grow after only a few months!

4. Using your brain rather than an app

With a little help, keeping track of your budget and savings objectives may be a lot easier! There are a slew of free applications and websites that will manage your spending and savings so you can keep track of every aspect of your budget and where every dollar is going.

Here are some resources to help you find the right app:

Digit aids in the automation of savings.

Investing options that you may do immediately from your phone

Apps to assist you in getting out of debt

5. Deferring high-interest debt

Ignoring high-interest debt, such as credit card debt, can end up costing you a lot of money in the long run. So, if you have debt to pay off, you should try to do so as soon as possible to save money on interest. The longer that you wait to pay off your debt, the more it will cost you.

But, at the same time, you should make sure you have some money in savings, because the last thing that you want to do in an emergency is charge it to a credit card.

As a result, it's critical to prioritize both. And here's how you can accomplish it: put half of any excess money you have each month toward debt and the other half into savings. Then, once you've built up a large emergency savings fund, devote all of that extra cash to paying down your high-interest debt. If you get a large chunk of money, such as a tax refund or a bonus at work, use it to pay down your debt.

You can have another approach to saving which is a daily approach

Some easy ways to save some money every day:

HOW TO SAVE MONEY

1. Schedule a "money date" once a week. Make it a compulsory to sit down with your money at least once a week for a money date. Update your budget, evaluate your accounts, and measure your progress toward your financial goals throughout this period. If you want to better your financial situation, you must spend time with your money, just like you would with any other relationship.

2. Make a week's worth of meal plans. Investing a few hours each weekend to food shop and meal prepare for the week will save your money, as dining out is the most expensive item for most families. You save money that would otherwise be spending on taxes and tips by eating at home—and you usually save calories as well.

3. Remove the cable. Gasp! What if you stopped watching TV? Never! You can now watch your favorite TV series and movies for a fraction of the cost of cable TV with services like Hulu, Netflix, and Amazon Prime.

Cable rates will soon rise to an average of $123 per month, or $1,476 per year, according to market research firm NPD Group. You can save money on other financial goals by switching to an online subscription or cutting off TV completely, such as paying off debt, vacationing, or saving for a down payment on a home.

4. Change to a pass programmed for exercising. A fitness pass programmed, such as Class Pass, is the way to go if you enjoy working out. You may visit many of the greatest studios in your area for $99 per month if you pay a membership fee. Cycling, yoga, Pilates, barre, weight training, boot camp, dancing, and other classes are all available. This is preferable to paying hundreds of dollars per month for each studio's monthly membership or individual class charge.

5. Organize a potluck. You spend more money on lunch dates, birthday parties, and gifts if you have a lot of friends.

HOW TO SAVE MONEY

Instead of meeting over a lavish dinner, throw a potluck and invite everyone to bring their favorite dish. You'll save money on restaurant expenses like tax, tip, and parking, and you'll usually have a more private meal together as a result.

6. Make use of vacation rental websites. Using a housing rental service like Airbnb, Travelmob, or Housetrip to find a place to stay while travelling is quite simple. At a budget comparable to hotels, you can often locate a room with a kitchen (so you can make meals at home to save money). While travelling, you may even rent out your own apartment on services like Airbnb to supplement your income and pay for your own travel expenditures. This is a win-win situation.

7. Brew your own coffee at home. This isn't my favorite because I enjoy visiting coffee shops and sipping wonderful organic coffee. Spending $4 to $5 on a coffee every day, on the other hand, adds up quickly. So, take my advice and buy coffee in cafes a few times a week while making it at home the rest of the time.

8. Put in extra effort. When you work a lot, you don't have much time to go shopping or spend money. So, keep yourself active and work in a field that you enjoy.

9. Do not click "purchase" until 48 hours have passed. Because we can get everything, we want with the press of a button these days, you'll need to find a method to assist you avoid impulse purchases.

For example, before spending money on items that cost more than a specific amount, wait 48 hours. When you do, you will notice that the item was usually more of a "desire" than the "need." You'll also save money & work toward becoming more and more frugal with your money.

10. Learn DIY beauty treatments from blogs and Pinterest. Self-care is crucial, but travelling to spas for pedicures,

massages, and other treatments can quickly add up. Allow yourself a certain amount to spend on these items, and then look for at-home beauty treatments on blogs and apps like Pinterest to help you save money. Often, a DIY organic option can be found utilizing basic household or kitchen items.

11. Be inventive with your gifts. With free, low-cost, or handcrafted birthday and holiday gifts, you may convey your love to friends and family in unique ways. After all, a handwritten message articulating why you love someone can be more meaningful than a pricey present that he or she may never use. Most people will value your thoughtfulness above all else, so don't be afraid to cut corners and discover free methods to commemorate birthdays and holidays.

12. Prioritize the quality of your work over the quantity. This can be applied to food, clothing, gadgets, and a variety of other items. Although it may be tempting to choose for the less expensive version of the item, selecting quality over quantity can save you money in the long term. Save your money and buy the highest-quality products that you can, then use the cost-per-wear principle to justify more expensive clothing and shoes.

This also applies to food: buying high-quality organic food can nourish you in ways that are more filling than packed, processed foods, and may save you money on future health-care costs because you're taking care of yourself. Find the balance for you and prioritize quality whenever its possible.

13. Work through your feelings. Excessive spending is frequently used as a means of avoiding certain feelings. If you check in with yourself before going on a big shopping spree, you might be able to figure out if you're bored, lonely, or stressed and are using money to distract yourself from the underlying emotion.

HOW TO SAVE MONEY

15. Forget about keeping up with Kardashians. It's difficult not to compare your money situation with others particularly celebrities. However, it is critical to be clear about what is most crucial to you and to create a financial strategy that helps and supports that goal. This will help you stay on track with your financial goals and will prevent you from overspending on things you don't need in order to impress individuals you don't like.

16. Read a book on personal finance. When you learn about personal finance, you'll discover even more ways to save money for your long-term goals. Knowledge is the power, and the more information you have, the more money you can save.

17. Maintain a healthy "FOMO/YOLO" mindset. People often fall victim to "fear of missing out" syndrome and instead go beyond with a "you only live once" mentality, with social media ruling our lives like never before.

While it is crucial to live in the moment and savior each wonderful moment, you must also save for your financial future. You may find yourself saying yes to everything and spending more money than you have due to a fear of missing out if you don't have checks and balances in place.

18. Create a list of your financial goals. Make your financial goals very specific. For example, saying "I want to save for a down payment on a house" isn't adequate. You'll need to work out how much you'll need, when you'll need it, and how much you'll need to save each month to achieve your objective. You'll be more likely to stick to your objectives and save for them in the long term if you know what they are.

19. Keep your focus on the goal. Make a list of the financial goals you want to achieve. Make a list of particular financial goals. "I'd like to save for a down payment on a house," for example, isn't sufficient. To attain your goal, you'll need to

HOW TO SAVE MONEY

figure out how much money you'll need, when you'll need it, and how much money you'll need to save each month. If you know what your long-term goals are, you'll be more inclined to stick to them and save for them.

Saving money can be simple and thrilling at first, but after a while, you may lose interest and begin to look for other ways to spend your money. Check-in with your goals on a frequent basis to stay on track and keep your sight on the prize.

20. Keep tabs on your development. Americans save barely 5.5 percent of their income, compared to the 20% recommended by personal finance experts. Rather than feeling guilty about your lack of savings, begin by saving something.

Even 1% is preferable to nothing. Keep note of your accomplishments and set a goal to increase your total each year. You can gradually build up to that 20% savings level, day by day.

The truth is that there are a variety of ways to save money. Find the ways that work best for you and implement them gradually into your regular routine.

As long as we earn enough money and don't overspend, we can live the life of our dreams. While the majority of us are obsessed with balancing our personal spending with a once-a-year trip to ensure we have a bed to sleep in and food to eat every day, many others are in control of their salaries and credit card debts! They put in the same effort that we do, but their cost-cutting technique has upped the ante.

Chapter 06

To save money, there are a few guidelines to follow

:

The Rule of 24 Hours:

The 24-hour rule is followed by millionaires. They may not need to think twice before making a large buy, but they do give it a day's thinking before making the final decision. Impulsive purchases are made as a result of an emotional impulse and are frequently needless. You won't splurge as much if you ask yourself the "desire or need" question.

An All-Cash Diet:

Cashless economies are great for your wallet, but they're not so great for credit card bills. Cash is preferred over a card by people who spend intelligently, especially for minor transactions. The wealthy make it a habit to stay out of debt as much as possible. To keep track of your costs, start paying for meals in cash and avoid recording your card information in browsers.

Set a Budget:

This may sound cliche, but making a clear budget and sticking to it every payday will help you save a lot of money. Make an honest "income vs. expenditure" audit and set a spending limit for yourself. It's referred to as the 50/30/20 budgeting strategy by financial gurus.

50% - Essentials

30% - Personal

20% - Savings

HOW TO SAVE MONEY

Spend on thing that help you earn:

You don't have to be unhappy in order to save money. The wealthy spend their money on items that will pay off in the long run. It's a good idea to make purchases that will help you with your work, contribute to your existing job, or increase your overall earning potential.

Kimberly Palmer, content to splurge on professional attire, a decent laptop, or a solid vehicle.

Spend money on services that will save you time.

According to Business Insider, the wealthy are not hesitant to spend money on services that will save them time and emotional anguish. Rather of spending, they concentrate on investment. Having your groceries delivered to your home, employing laundry services, or renting a more expensive apartment to be closer to work will all contribute to the quality of your life. These things may be more expensive, but they provide you with more time to accomplish the things that make you happy.

Experiences are priceless.

Millionaires live a flamboyant lifestyle and make it a point to fill their calendars with life events. This is because they place a high value on meaningful experiences that improve their lives and health. They would gladly substitute life-changing expeditions, skydiving, trips, or a gym membership for their daily expenses!

First, pay your bills, then relax!

Understanding your fixed expenses is something that people who are good with money do better than the rest of us. They swear by paying their set expenses using automatic systems on the first of the month so they can see where the rest of their money is going.

HOW TO SAVE MONEY

Make a buying list for the upcoming holiday discounts.

We all enjoy bargains. Buying items that aren't on sale, on the other hand, does not always imply saving money. As appealing as sales can seem, they eventually lead you to overspend and purchase items that you didn't require in the first place. People who are good with money recommend making a shopping list ahead of time and scheduling significant purchases during sales to get a big bargain.

Invest on things that bring you joy and keep you healthy.

It's fine to buy things that make you happy and contribute to your interests and passions every now and again. The wealthy "work hard and play hard" by making sure they enjoy their occupations and investing in things that make them happy.

Splurging on a telescope if you're passionate about constellations is fine as long as your savings allow it and you're truly satisfied.

Begin with "no-spend" days or weekends.

People who are skilled at saving are also good at resisting the need to spend more than they have. Try having a "no spending" day every week or on weekends and adhering to it.

Save your money and invest it wisely.

Loose change is something that everyone despises. You forget about a coin once you've dropped it in your bag. But here's the thing: every penny you save is a dime you make! To reduce your everyday spending to a minimum, keep your change accessible and reuse it for your coffee/snack breaks.

Things should be repaired before being discarded.

While the wealthy like investing, they believe in sticking to their decisions until their dying breath. They promote the idea of having technology and gadgets fixed rather than discarded when they break down.

Chapter 07

Let's see now, how you can stop spending the saved money:

Money, whether we like it or not, is what keeps the world turning. We spend money for a variety of reasons, and if we're being honest, a lot of them can be traced back to our current mood. This is where things get a little dicey—and overspending can result.

When it comes to spending money, there are five major red flags to be aware of:

1. Use of social media

Social media, oh, social media, oh, social media, o I despise to adore and despise to despise social media. Consider the following scenario: It's Saturday morning, and you're browsing through your social media feed, trying to keep up with what your friends are up to.

If you're being honest, you probably didn't have to think too hard to conjure up that situation this morning. Let's face it: we all desire what we lack. And we desire it because we believe it will improve our lives.

However, social media intensifies the comparison game. Your couch looks like it was picked up from the side of the road after your friend posted about their brand-new couch with those gorgeous toss cushions. And that well-known blogger's piece about the fantastic all-inclusive resort she visited makes your recent family vacation look like a trip to the state fair. When will it be over?

2. You don't keep track of your expenses

No matter how much money you make (or don't make), if you don't track your spending, you'll never be in control of your finances. In fact, you'll have the feeling that your money owns you at all times.

It's no secret that living paycheck to paycheck is a dreadful experience. And if you're always wondering where your hard-earned money goes each month, it's time to start tracking it... with a budget!

If you stick with me, I'll show you how.

3. Shopping to Improve Your Mood

Some people joke about shopping like a shopaholic, but compulsive shopping, often known as retail therapy, is a serious condition.

The problem for most of us is that we spend money on impulse merely because we want something now. We see something and buy it before we evaluate our bank account balance (or before considering our financial goals, for that matter). Instant satisfaction isn't always what it seems. It doesn't make you feel any better... especially when your bank account is dwindling in front of your eyes.

4. Inadequate self-awareness

Gaining self-awareness is the one thing that has made a significant difference in my money perspective. It will be all too simple for an old habit or an "easy" out to creep in and wreck my progress if I don't continue to learn about myself and be mindful of my money habits (I call them pendency's).

You must have a good understanding of yourself to determine what might tempt you and what you should avoid. Are you naturally more of a spender or a saver? Do you think of yourself as a nerd or a free thinker?

HOW TO SAVE MONEY

Which is more important to you: safety or status? Take my free quiz to learn why you handle money the way you do and how to permanently eliminate harmful money habits.

5. Using Plastic to Pay

You may not realize it, but when you pay with plastic, whether it's a credit card (who doesn't like purchasing with someone else's money?) or a debit card, you probably spend more. Consider this: When you shop with plastic, it's easy to overspend since you can't see your money leave your hand.

Chapter 08

Spending Habits:

When you spend cash, though, you can feel it. It aches when those crisp (or wadded up) green bills go from your grasp. Something makes you squirm within. You had money just seconds ago—and now? You don't have it. So, the next time you make a transaction, pay cash and you'll see what I'm talking about.

The good news is that you can break these spending habits with some forethought, self-awareness, and long-term thinking.

1. Do your shopping on Wednesdays.

What distinguishes a Wednesday from the rest of the week? Many grocery stores launch new promotions and discounts in the middle of the week, generally on Wednesdays, so shoppers who walk the aisles then are often the first to discover about new deals. Additionally, most stores recognize coupons from the previous week. Most significantly, you may maximize your discounts by buying during a less busy weekday.

2. Trade.

Mary Kaarto, an author and former editor in Missouri City, Texas, recalls going through two layoffs as a single mother years ago – and having to stretch her dollars as far as she could. So, she made a deal. Her hairstylist, for example, was a first-time mother. Kaarto needed to look her best for job interviews, and the hairstylist needed someone she could

HOW TO SAVE MONEY

trust to care for her infant when she and her husband went on date evenings. Kaarto would get her hair styled and babysit at no charge. It was a win-win situation for her and her hairstylist, she claims.

3. Keep advertising on your computer.

Instead of making impulse purchases, you may save adverts or computer images of items you want, or keep a list of links to purchases you want to make later.

Kaarto claims to keep a file of classified advertising not only for herself but also for family members. What is it about advertisements that fascinates people?

Kaarto's advertising, on the other hand, give her gift ideas for birthdays and the holidays, allowing her to buy things that her family actually wants or needs, while her own ads save her money.

"What I've realized through delayed gratification is that I save money in one way or another," Kaa

adds.

4. Create a savings account for any unexpected income or presents.

Even if you're past the age of getting birthday money from relatives, you may still receive an unexpected sum of money. According to Miguel Suro, a Miami-based attorney who co-founded the personal finance website RichMiser.com with his wife, Lily Rodriguez, if you set up a separate savings account specifically for unexpected income, you might be astonished at how much money you end up with.

Suro suggests, "Deposit all unexpected income there." "I'm referring about refunds for product recalls, class action settlements, refunds you get when you return an item, and money you receive as a gift." It's just money that you hadn't budgeted for or expected.

5. Try the $5 trick.

Aimee Spencer Tiemann, a Detroit-based writer, claims that a few years ago, her best friend shared a money-saving tip with her: "Every time she got $5, whether it was change from a purchase or tips as a bartender, she put it in a jar at her house. She responded definitely that she would put $5 in the container if she received it. At the end of a year, she had $4,000 in her account."

Spencer Tiemann claims she did the same thing and earned $1,200 in three months. "It's strange how something as simple as setting aside a certain amount of money can elicit a psychological response in your brain. You're not pondering anything. You simply have to do it. It's almost as if you're playing a video game "she clarifies

With that stated, if you don't usually carry cash, you might want to check out Acorns, Chime, or another app that will round up your debit or credit card transactions and deposit them into a savings account. Although some of these apps are paid, you should save substantially more than you spend if you use them. Acorns charges $1 per year for accounts under $5,000, while Chime, a mobile bank app, charges nothing save a $2.50 out-of-network ATM fee.

6. Use the traditional coin-saving approach.

Granted, with a national coin scarcity, it's been a little more difficult to save coins recently, but Spencer Tiemann says she's been saving her change for the past year and putting it in a jar. It's been going swimmingly for her.

"It didn't take long for the money saved from grocery stores and carryout to build up. Of course, I don't want to be blamed for our country's currency shortage "Spencer Tiemann argues that storing coins has been beneficial to her. "If I tallied it all up, I'd have more than doubled my emergency money."

7. Make the envelope system a part of your life.

You can pay for everything in cash with this method. "I'm not sure if this is creative or just old-school," confesses Kristine Thorndyke, CEO of Test Prep Nerds, a company that provides test prep materials for examinations such as the MCAT.

Thorndyke claims she and her boyfriend saved money early in her career when they were establishing their firm and were cash-strapped by paying for everything in cash. They were literally withdrawing cash for their monthly budget and depositing the determined amounts into envelopes designated for each area, such as grocery, entertainment, apartment, gym, and miscellaneous, according to her.

8. Set a goal for yourself to reuse as much as possible.

You might be able to repurpose some of your junk if you start challenging yourself to pause before throwing out trash. Consider the plastic sandwich bag in which you placed a sandwich and are going to discard the bag after the food has been consumed. There are a few crumbs, but what else? Maybe you could wash it and use it when it dries the next day?

Sure, it sounds cheap, and your family will certainly mock you – but if you save money on items like plastic bags and aluminum foil (how much of that do you toss away when you could just wash it off, dry it off, smooth it out, and use it again?) you'll save money in the long run. You might get a few appreciative glances if you do your part to help the environment.

9. Shop at secondhand stores for clothing.

Jodi O'Donnell-Ames, the founder of Hope Loves Company Inc. in Pennington, New Jersey, an organization that provides education and emotional support to children and young people with ALS family members, says she stopped buying new clothes a long time ago. She now only shops at thrift and consignment stores.

She says, "I can't begin to tell you how much money this little task has saved me."

If you despise the thought of purchasing secondhand apparel, O'Donnell-Ames has some suggestions: "I often purchase products that are brand new with tags and cost one-eighth of the original price. The clothing, on the other hand, are brand new."

10. Inquire about a sale on an item.

Because we're all focused on Googling offers, we forget about this strategy, says Charles Thomas, a financial counsellor and the founder of Intrepid Eagle Finance in Charlotte, North Carolina.

11. Take a vacation where you don't have to spend any money.

Choose a day or two – or a week if you can – and promise not to spend any money other than your monthly bills. It's all too easy to overspend at the supermarket or on Amazon's impulsive buys. However, if you begin to plan your own no-spend vacations, you may be able to retrain your brain to spend less.

Chapter 09

How to Turn Saving Money into an Addiction

You can develop a saving habit with practice.

You can develop a saving habit with practice.

Shopping, without a doubt, may become an addiction, a significant problem that can jeopardize your financial security. Did you know, though, that saving money can become addictive? It appears that way our brains work determines whether we become addicted to spending or saving.

HAPPINESS HORMONES:

The "happy hormone" is a hormone that causes people to feel good.

When we experience pleasure, whether it is as a result of spending or conserving money, something happens: Dopamine is a neurotransmitter released by our brains. When we receive a reward, this "happy hormone" is released. A new purchase may be the reward for one individual, while saving money or making a new investment may provide the same pleasure for another.

And this is where addiction enters the picture: the better we feel each time we spend or save, the more inclined we are to seek that same "high" again.

So, if you're a spender who want to be a saver, what should you do? You can take the following five steps:

HOW TO SAVE MONEY

1. Refrain from acting on your impulses.

You must first train your brain to quit spending impulsively before you can teach it to save money. Leave your debit card, credit cards, and checkbook at home unless you're going out to get things you need to live (like groceries). Only take as much money as you're willing to part with. Take enough cash to purchase a coffee and go to lunch if a friend asks you to go shopping. You won't lose out on anything crucial if you don't need anything to begin with, even if you walk into a store filled with wonderful sales.

Among these top picks, find the finest stock broker for you. You'll find a stockbroker to suit your trading needs, whether you're looking for a unique sign-up deal, excellent customer service, zero commissions, smart mobile apps, or more.

Stop receiving catalogues and flyers from your favorite retailers. Disable one-click ordering on your computer and unsubscribe from communications. Create stumbling hurdles to spending, or "friction," as behavioral economists call it. Slowing down for a few seconds will often give you enough time to reconsider an impulse purchase.

2. Prepare yourself with information.

According to an Ally Bank poll, saving money has a greater impact on happiness than earning money. Having money in the bank, according to 84 percent of those polled, was more significant than having a job they enjoy, getting regular exercise, or eating healthy foods in contributing to their overall sense of well-being.

Money may not be able to buy happiness, but it can help your mental health by reducing stress and boosting confidence. Having money set up gives you options. You can save, invest, travel, return to school, retire earlier, start a new interest, or just quit a job that is draining your energy and find one that better matches your skills.

HOW TO SAVE MONEY

Knowing these facts alone may not be enough to change your mind, but knowledge can serve as a guide. If you're tempted to spend money you don't have, ask yourself: Would I rather have this thing right now, or would I rather feel safer and more confident in the future?

The goal is to change your perspective on shopping. You can either give your money to a firm and let them become wealthy, or you can keep it and let it work for you.

3. Give yourself a reward

That dopamine rush is what you're going for. It takes practice to achieve the same level of satisfaction in saving as you did in spending. Here are some ideas about how you might practice:

When you're tempted to buy something, tell yourself that if you still want it, you can have it in 24 hours. Then either exit the store or turn off the computer. Take a few minutes to sit with yourself and think about how you're feeling. You're probably pleased with yourself. As the hours pass, you'll probably find that your life is just great without the item you almost purchased.

Keep a diary. Make a list of everything you didn't buy. Make careful to include the amount you saved in your calculations. Add up your savings at the end of the week. How does it feel to reclaim control once more?

Make your savings automatic. Request that your bank or credit union deposit money into your savings account automatically every time you get paid. Examine your account balances at least once a month to see how they've grown. Give yourself a pat on the back for being a responsible person.

4. Educate yourself on investing

HOW TO SAVE MONEY

Learn everything you can about investment and how it may benefit you. Make a list of all the reasons you deserve to be financially secure in your mind. The more you read, the more you'll want to put money into your future.

When you go beyond simply saving and learn how to invest your money, you'll find that the stock market gives better long-term returns, albeit there are no guarantees. Check out these online stock brokers for plenty of research and inexpensive (or free) charges and fees.

5. Take your time.

You didn't develop a buying addiction overnight, and you won't develop a saving addiction overnight. Each happy emotion you have, each dopamine rush, makes it easier to do the right thing the following time. The idea is to practice until you crave the sense of accomplishment that comes from putting money in your savings account.

Choosing the wrong broker might cost you a lot of money.

There has never been a better method to enhance your wealth in the long run than through investing in the stock market. However, choosing the wrong broker might significantly reduce your investment returns. Our experts have researched and reviewed the best online stock brokers; simply click here to see the results and discover how to take advantage of our top-rated brokers' free trades and cash bonuses.

Why is Consistency the Main Aspect of Saving Money?

It makes no difference what your annual income is. Saving money should be a top priority at all times. Even more so when you're on a shoestring budget. Saving money is a difficult task. People are frequently unable to save and even spend more than they earn.

HOW TO SAVE MONEY

While there are times when you spend more than you earn owing to high living costs or other unforeseen costs (family concerns, health issues, etc.), there are also times when you spend more than you earn due to high living costs or other unforeseen costs (family matters, health issues, etc.). A significant proportion of people borrow money to acquire goods they don't truly need.

The difficulty is that even when you have more money, your conduct does not change. It becomes a personality feature that spirals your financial condition "down below" deeper and deeper.

finance for climate change

It's natural to believe that saving money is simpler when you have a lot of it, and this is true to some level. I agree that saving money on a limited budget is more difficult, but you must begin there. People start modest, or at least in most situations, and through time, they are able to collect greater money.

But, you know, you've got to start somewhere, right?

It is always necessary to take the initial step. That is often the only thing standing between you and a monetary cushion that can help you sleep easier at night.

However, there is a snag... It is not enough to simply begin saving money; you must continue to do so. That is the most important factor.

All you have to do now is keep going. After your payday, you will always save. As a result, you must be diligent 12 times a year. However, if you want your money to last, you must be very frugal every day and look for ways to acquire free money.

Consider placing the money you've saved in a separate account that you don't check all the time. Definitely put on

HOW TO SAVE MONEY

an account with no direct debit card access. Make the journey to your saved money a little more difficult so you don't spend it all at once.

Because the more money you save, the more you'll begin to consider what you can buy with it. Many possibilities will appear out of nowhere, attempting to swindle you out of your money.

Always remember how long it took you to get to this figure and how good it feels to save money at such times. Usually, after you've had it, you won't want to give it away easily.

Saving money, like so many other things, must become a habit. As if it were second nature. After 30 days, habits begin to build. When you think how much of an influence it may have on your life, it doesn't seem like much.

The earlier you begin, the more money you will save. You will be able to repay debt and invest more if you have more money. Increasing the value of your financial future.

Chapter 10

How To Save Money and Accumulate More Wealth

Financial independence comes to those who can save 10% or more of their income throughout the course of their lives.

Developing the practice of saving a portion of your money, every paycheck, is one of the smartest things you can do for yourself.

Individuals, families, and even entire communities are more stable and affluent when they save money. Today's savings are what ensure the security and possibilities of the future.

Here are four strategies to help you save money and build wealth.

First and foremost, pay yourself.

The first corollary of the Law of Savings and how to become a money-saving expert comes from George Classon's book The Richest Man in Babylon. "Pay yourself first," as the saying goes.

Start saving ten percent of your wages right now, off the top, and don't touch it. This is your long-term investment money, and you never use it for anything other than securing your financial future.

HOW TO SAVE MONEY

The amazing thing is that if you pay yourself first and force yourself to survive on the remaining 90% of your income, you will quickly become acclimated to it.

You're a creature of habit, aren't you?

When you save 10% of your income on a regular basis, you'll soon be able to live comfortably on the remaining 90%. Many people begin by saving 10% of their salary and gradually increase their savings to 15%, 20%, and even more. As a result, their financial lives shift substantially. Yours will, too.

2) Make Use Of Tax-Advantaged Savings And Investment Accounts

"Take advantage of tax-deferred savings and investment programs," states the second corollary of the Law of Savings and becoming a money-saving expert.

Money that is saved or invested without being taxed increases faster than money that is taxed due to high and even multiple tax rates.

According to Dr. Thomas Stanley's book "The Millionaire Next Door," self-made billionaires are virtually obsessed with accumulating wealth in assets like real estate, self-owned businesses, and securities that increase in value without generating tax penalties.

Invest in business pension and retirement plans, 401(k) plans, Roth IRAs, Education Investment Accounts, stock option programs, and any other long-term financial accumulation vehicle approved by the IRS.

Make each and every penny count!

How to Increase Your Wealth

I'd like to share two strategies with you that you may start implementing in your life right now to start generating more wealth.

10% of your earnings should be set aside.

First, start putting away 10% of your earnings now. Set up a separate account for this purpose, and regard your contributions to it with the same care you do your monthly rent or mortgage payments.

Become a student of how to save money for the rest of your life.

Second, commit to learning how to save money for the rest of your life. Take courses, read the best books, and subscribe to the most useful magazines. Know what you're doing so you can make informed judgments when it comes to investing your money.

"Financial freedom comes to the person who actively takes control of their finances."

Saving Money on Tight Budget:

1. Change the way you use electricity.

Your electric company may provide free tools to help you assess your home's energy usage and recommend strategies to reduce your consumption and lower your cost. If you aren't on a time-of-use plan and it is available where you live, for example, switching to one could save you money. If you are, adjusting when you use energy-intensive equipment like laundry dryers, washers, and dishwashers could help you save money.

2. Determine if you are eligible for low-income utility assistance.

The federal Low Income Home Energy Assistance Program collaborates with states to assist low-income families in staying warm in the winter and cool in the summer.

The federal Low Income Home Energy Assistance Program collaborates with states to assist low-income families in staying warm in the winter and cool in the summer. The qualifications and levels of support for aid with heating and cooling expenditures vary by state. Some programs will even assist you weatherize your home to save money on energy expenses or replace a damaged furnace or boiler.

3. Before hiring a professional, do a YouTube search.

Some jobs are too perilous to attempt on your own. If you try to solve an issue yourself, you can make it worse and cost you more money in the long run.

However, after watching someone else complete a work, we may find that it is shockingly inexpensive and simple to complete ourselves. Do some video research first the next time you have a problem that you'd ordinarily pay a professional to handle, whether it's changing your car's air filter or replacing your oven's heating element.

HOW TO SAVE MONEY

4. Make the switch to a prepaid phone plan.

When it comes to cellphone providers, most of us think of the big three: T-Mobile, Verizon, and AT&T. Their recurring monthly plans, on the other hand, are pricey and may include more data, quicker speeds, and newer phone technology than you require.

You might be able to decrease your monthly price in half if you switch to one of their prepaid plans. Switching to a smaller carrier like Republic Wireless, Ting, or Mint Mobile can also help you save money. Paying in advance for at least three months of service is also an option. If you don't use cellular data and instead rely on talking, texting, and Wi-Fi, you can save a lot of money on your plan.

5. Allocate one subscription to yourself

Newspapers. Television, movies, and music are all sources of entertainment. Cloud storage is a method of storing data on the cloud Photo retouching Processing of text. Exercise classes are available. These days, it seems like every firm has a subscription-based revenue model. It's a terrific way to make money if you can get someone to join up for a service and pay for it in the long run.

Which one of your subscriptions do you utilize the most? Allow yourself that indulgence, and then reduce the rest of your calories. Many of them have no-cost alternatives. You also don't have to commit to a single subscription for the entire year. You can change it up for anything that is on a month-to-month basis: This month, Hulu, next month, Netflix, and the month after that, Spotify.

Conclusion

To conclude this, the thing to remember along the process of saving money is that you need consistency in this process. As this is not the process that someone will enjoy. So, make sure that you reward yourself along the way and think about the reward that you will earn in the end. This will keep you motivated.

Make sure that you follow the advises given in the book. Whether you are making an extra money or whether you are saving a buck from the salary you have, make sure to do it consistently as well. I hope you have a good journey along the way.

Stop reading and start saving now.

HOW TO SAVE MONEY

Conclusion

So, that's the last of it for the time being, I hope. Please accept my genuine hope that this resource has offered you with at least a few valuable tidbits of knowledge. Thank you for reading my eBook. As previously said, a great relationship is the result of a lot of distinct factors coming together, including work on partners' parts, uniqueness, imagination, and, of course, courage (to name a few).

Keep a journal of your observations on what works best for you and what causes you the most trouble. The first and most important thing to remember is that you can't expect to be the greatest at everything, therefore try a variety of different activities.

Because each woman will have different expectations and interests, you will need to tailor your approach to meet their needs and interests accordingly. Although this is the case, many well-known key foundations will continue to exist in their existing configuration.

Ultimately, you should follow your instincts and you'll be OK. Every successful relationship is built on a foundation of mutual trust and honesty between the two persons involved in the partnership.

When two people are linked in this manner, the foundation on which their love may flourish is being established.

In today's world, it's easy to lose sight of what the word "love" really means in its most basic sense.

Because of the seemingly never-ending list of everyday concerns that we confront on a daily basis, we may quickly get distracted and bored in our job. But be assured those genuine relationships do exist; all that is required is a certain level of work and attention on your part in order for them to blossom into something lasting.

Never forget that there is someone out there who is right for you – and that she is almost certainly looking for you at the same time as you are searching for her. It fills me with dread to think of losing out on such a beautiful relationship and allowing the chance of a lifetime to slide through your fingers and into the hands of someone else.

It's important to take a step back and consider what you actually want out of life, which I encourage to all single people.

Consider reevaluating your dating-related aims and beliefs, and then comparing them to the activities you do daily to achieve those ambitions and beliefs, and vice versa.

In the event that you and your partner are experiencing a gap in your relationship, you may want to consider making some adjustments to the way you approach love and dating in the future.

Increasing your awareness of your own behaviors and how they could be seen by others will make the aim much more feasible.

Try to imagine what it would be like to walk a mile in someone else's shoes for a day or a week.

Reconsider your position and consider things from a different viewpoint. Invest some time in self-reflection and introspection.

"Will you have any regrets when your life story has been written?" is a question that is often put to individuals by others.

HOW TO SAVE MONEY

Printed in Great Britain
by Amazon